MW01644905

I NEED ACCESS TO MY CHILDREN

A PARENT'S GUIDE TO REGAINING ACCESS TO THEIR CHILDREN AFTER A SEPARATION

DR. MICHAEL BISONG

Printed in the United States of America

First Printing Edition, 2024

I S B N 979-88842617-9-2

Dedication

This book is dedicated to my dear parents, children, and grandchildren.

Acknowledgment

I acknowledge everyone who has been influential and supportive in my life.

Writing this book has been very challenging but even more rewarding. This would not have been possible without the support and encouragement of Danielle Mantho. I wholeheartedly thank Down Ghostwriting for countless hours of editing and facilitating the publishing process.

Sincere thanks to Dr. Francis Mutajuka (RIP) and his wife, Dr. Carol Mutajuka, Mr. Mathias Mudoh, Lady Grace Elone, Mr. Cyrille Makanaky, Charlie Nzams, Mr. Zepa Alessane, Mr. Simon Nlend, Coach Jean-Pierre Sadi, Mr. Joseph Kamga, Mr. Tabi Darah (Cameroon Football Legends), Mr. Stephen Bessong (Coach), Mr. Jacques Wolani, Mr. & Mrs. Sumelong, Esambe Rudolph Ebot, Dr. Charles Nche, Dr. Nkongho-nyoh Adolph (RIP), Barrister Nzo Tarh and wife, Dr. Rachael Eben, Dr. Thomas Eben, Dr. Mathias Chiano, Mr. Phillip Eben, Mr. Ebeny Amstrong, Mr. Aaron Bisong (RIP), Mr. Simon Didier (AKA Papiss), Mr. Joe Takor and wife, Rev Apostle Mary Stella, Mr. Hardison Chukwu, Mr. Ralph Tanyi, Mr. Chris Nasah, Wilson Lache (AKA Bosco), and Mr. Gervase Fuh (AKA Tchebo) for being the most influential and role models in my life.

Special thanks to my lovely parents, Pa John Bisong and Mme Regina Atong Bisong (both RIP). They showered me with constant love, support, and guidance, and I can proudly say I would not be the person I am today without them. To my brother Maurice Bisong (AKA BB - RIP), known as an intellect. He taught me how to read and write from a very young age, which I can proudly say I benefitted from to a great extent. To my uncle, Teacher Eben Abraham (RIP). He provided me with early education opportunities by enrolling me in his school to kick off my education. To my sister Marie Bisong. She took over the mantle of a mother at a very young age and ensured my entire basic healthcare and educational needs were met.

To my grandfather Tabi John Bisong, AKA Manawa (RIP). Thank you so much for always being there with a smile and a kind word, coupled with strict discipline. Your presence in my life was a gift. Your wisdom and guidance shaped me into the person I am today. I am forever grateful for the love you showed not only to me but to the entire family, who continue to remember you and talk so well of you. You were truly a role model to us all, and the legacy you left behind will forever be remembered.

To sister Rosemary Bisong, Ma Mary Ediang Tarh (RIP), Pa Enow (RIP), Pa John Bisong (RIP), Pa Aaron Bisong and wife Mami Beltha Arrey Bisong, both (RIP), Pa Hans Awah (RIP), Mme Martha Bechem (RIP), Ashu Thompson Nat, Sister Helen Taku, Solomon Eben Tabi AKA Doctor (RIP) Sister Sophie Eben Tabi (RIP), Sister Helen Eben Tabi (RIP), Peter Eben Tabi (RIP), Martha Bechem, Regina Bisong, Bisong Lucas Tarh (RIP), Mary Enow Bisong (RIP), Pellagie Bisong Ayuk-Tabi, Isabela Atong Tarh (mother), Pelagie Ayuk Eben, Takang Genabelle Nkeng, Barrister Sylvie Awah, Lieutenant Commander William Eben Nkongho, Francis Eben, Hans Awah, Benarly Atong Eben, Tecla Tarh, Gilbert Tanyi Bisong, Joyce Neh Bisong (RIP), Emilia Bisong (RIP), Bebe Nchung (RIP), Santana Tabi, Barbara Misodi, Mustapha Tabi, Rosemary Ngute, Pegsol Tarkoh, Livancliff Nfongang, Emilien Enow, Aggie Enow, to all my aunties, uncles, nieces, and nephews and every other family member I have not mentioned. I thank you all for being a kind and supportive family.

To Mrs. Glory Ako Tambe, Mrs. Marriane Enow Tabi, Mr. Yanick Eyong Tambe, Mrs. Cecilia Tabe, Mme. Lydia Kuate Ayuk,

Martha Eyere Bakia, Mr. Benjamin Tambe, Margaret Tanyi, Mr. Valentine Ako, Mr. Ben Ako, Mrs Queen Iva, Mrs Hermine Kinyock, Louise Mahop, Mariama Charles, Hawa Charles, Mr Edward Eimhagwe, Mr Kelvin Njuhsop, Mr. Franklin Sone Bayern, Mr. Soter Agbaw Ebai, Isabel Arrey-Oben, Florina Chening, Larissa Chening, Mr Michael Chening, Mr. Francis Ngwa, Mr Kewssie Nkem, Elizabeth Betow, Mr. Eric Nfoh, Mr. Nobert Karngong, Mr. Jean Black Ngodi, Mr. Jean Ngeka, Dr. Stephen Bolla, Dr. Maurille Feudjo, Mr. Blaise Tchuisseu, Maître Claude Tene, Mr. Crosby Tagoe, Mr. Patrick Mandengue, and Mr. Michel Yemelong, thank you for your amazing love and support.

I am eternally grateful to all members of the Bisong Foundation in Cameroon and the UK, my Cambridge family, and the Veterans of the United Kingdom (VUKA) for their constant love and support.

To Jo Wilkins, Moji Odewusi, Flavia Sentamu, May Malm, Nqobile Nkomo, Taffie Chirodwodza, Brian Kotelo, Sylvia Anutika-Duval, Liz Hughes, Steven Flux, Sarah Ballantyne, Mary Munns, Val Howard, Kursten Mence, Michelle Chaonza, and Francis Gbedema, a big thank you for your immense support in my professional career development.

To all the orphans and carers my charity is supporting, to all the players and Management Team of the Bisong Football Academy, thank you for giving me the opportunity to put the biggest smiles on your faces and for positively impacting your lives.

Many thanks to my children and grandchildren, Endurance Bisong, Raul Bisong, Michael Jr Atong Bisong, Kibeya Oben, Kenlord Oben, Charles Ayuk, Abigail Tabe, Monika Mbibowo, A'Sharia Bisong-Dean, and Theo Bisong-Nicols for being the source of my happiness, strength and inspiration.

To Professor Bishop Faustina Clarke, Professor Bishop Heyford, and Professor Julie Hammond, sincere thanks for your support, guidance, and coaching toward my PhD success.

Special thanks to all my football/soccer friends, past and present, for sharing the good and bad moments of the game.

To my friends Epee et Koum (Legendary Artists of Cameroon), thank you so much for your brotherly love and support.

Special thanks to Mark (name changed) for providing his heartwarming story.

About the Author

Dr. Michael Bisong is a social worker with the Local Government Authority in the United Kingdom. He has worked for different teams and recorded multiple career successes. Many young people who have experienced separation or divorce have worked with Michael and received his emotional and practical support. Michael has also supported individuals going through a separation to gain access to their children successfully.

He is an ex-football/soccer player who represented Cameroon at the junior level and played semi-professional football in Europe before injury cut short his brilliant football career. However, he has kept this dream alive by personally supporting kids in football. He is also a philanthropist, CEO, and founder of the Bisong Foundation, a charitable not-for-profit organization dedicated to helping underprivileged children access quality education and primary healthcare. The charity also raises awareness about domestic violence and knife crimes in the UK with the objective of saving lives.

Contents

CHAPTER ONE

WHY CAN'T I ACCESS MY CHILDREN

This is one question I hope you'll never have to answer. Although we all understand that *life happens* and we must always expect the unexpected, you're never really prepared for when they do occur. What happens when everything you have worked so hard for suddenly comes to a grinding halt? How do you make peace with your dreams crumbling before your eyes? How do you accept that your life has been a façade and things will never work out how you expected? These are some of the many questions we may ask ourselves when life puts us on the spot, even more so when it involves the people we hold dear.

Building a family is the single most fulfilling experience for most parents. So fulfilling that it is almost impossible to think of what happens if there is a separation. No one prays for this to happen, but it does happen too often. It becomes worse when there are children involved. In most cases, these children become victims of circumstance and experience life-long effects on their mental, spiritual, and emotional journey. Also, it doesn't help that in some cultures and countries, specific genders are given more power over others. All things considered, separation remains a hard pill to swallow.

For everyone involved, a separation can be the most stressful and emotionally draining event they have ever endured. It is beyond devastating to witness the end of your marriage, the breakup of your family and seeing your children taken away from you. What also makes the situation unbearable for some parents is that following a divorce in most countries, child custody is granted to a primary parent. Children are, therefore, most likely to remain with primary parents after a divorce. Consequently, the alienated parent will only access their children through contact rights, court arrangements or cordial arrangements with the primary parent. Sometimes, even after a court order arrangement, the primary parent of the children may still deny the alienated parent access to their children. They sometimes do this as retribution for the separation. This, however, has untold effects on the overall wellbeing of the children.

One Friday, I arrived later than usual to pick up my son from school due to traffic. Upon arriving there, I was surprised to find another child with my son. Apparently, he was my son's classmate. What caught my attention was not that he was still in school at that time but because he looked very distressed and angry. As a parent and a social worker, I tried to find out why he was upset, but the little boy was so upset that he refused to utter a word. I insisted, but he decided to stay quiet. So, I decided to leave him alone and left with my son. On our way home, I turned my curiosity to my son and asked him if he knew why his classmate looked so frustrated. I was very surprised to hear that the source of this six-year-old boy's frustration was his parents' divorce. I was surprised that such a little boy could be so affected by his parents' divorce. I learned that his parents had been fighting for over two years. Unknown to them, they had created deeply rooted emotional turmoil for the child. The little boy couldn't understand why he had to travel between two homes. At the time of this incident, he had lost daily contact with one parent, had changed schools, and now lived with the primary parent who had full child custody. He now had challenges copping in school, his performances were poor, and he was becoming more aggressive with his teachers and classmates. Just the fact that this little boy could share all that was going on with his friends can tell you how deeply he was affected by the situation.

According to statistics, most children who grow up with a single parent end up becoming radical, joining gangs, and making terrible decisions that affect their future negatively. They are often impulsive, delinquent, and guilty of improper conduct. Therefore, children must grow up with the affection of both parents, even after a divorce. Doing this will ensure that the children gain a rounded and grounded understanding of cooperative co-parenting and are emotionally closer to both parents.

Accessing your children after a separation may seem like a dream, especially when you do not know the right thing to do. Sometimes, your desperation may even aggravate the process. I understand. I can talk about this only because I've been in this situation before, and I eventually worked out a strategy that worked for both parties. Similarly, I have also helped many struggling parents regain access to their children in a way that protects the interest of the child in question. Before we learn more about what a parent can do to gain legal access to their children in the subsequent chapter, let's follow closely what Mark has been going through in his statement below to have access to his children.

"My name is Mark, and I am the father of the children who are subject to this statement below:"

- Since 2006, I have attended several courts, including Family and High courts, in the search to establish a father and son relationship.

- Before the High Court, the following proceedings were running at the same time:
  - Declaration of Parentage Application.
  - Contact Application.
  - Application for Residence.
  - Application to have the birth certificates changed to reflect as biological father.
  - Application to have the children's middle and surnames changed.
  - Application for a Child Assessment Order by the BT.
  - Care Order Application by the BT.
  - In addition, an allegation of rape made by the children's mother arose after the Court ordered DNA testing, which proved that I was the biological father.
- This is the third time I am returning to the court because my children's mother refuses to allow contact as ordered by the Court.
- On 17th June 2014, the Court again ordered me to have contact with my children, namely unsupervised contact once per month for 2 hours.
- I was ill and did not attend the proceedings scheduled for 17 June 2014.
- The solicitor at the time informed me that he had withdrawn from the case when I tried to get the outcome from the proceedings a few weeks later.

- I had to pay the solicitor to get my contact order from the high court a few months later.

- On all birthdays and Christmas, I posted cards and presents, sometimes via the Social Services department.

- My sister in Cameroon called my ex-spouse on several occasions, but she didn't answer.

- I asked a friend who lived in the same city as my ex-spouse to speak to her via the phone. However, the response was that they should not get involved, and my friend was not to phone her again.

- I was advised to write to my ex-spouse and ask for forgiveness for any wrongdoing. I did, but I still had no success.

- Before that, I tried mediation, where two other ladies, on separate occasions, consulted with my ex-spouse to ask if she could allow me to see my children peacefully. However, she declined.

- In December 2016, I spoke to the boys privately and explained why it was difficult for me to meet them as before. I took their phone numbers and gave them my email address.

- In 2017, I tried to call my ex-spouse several times, but she did not respond, and I later noticed she had blocked my phone number on all her phones.

- Before Easter 2017, I went to her shop with the children's Easter presents. I was hoping to use this opportunity also to try to reunite with my children, but my ex-spouse called the police and made some allegations against me. The police ordered me not to visit her shop again and to consult my lawyer for further advice.

- I connected with my children on social media, and the letter from the court was posted to their mother, but she blocked me on her phone. Since then, I have been trying to return to the court but have not been able to raise the money needed to hire a lawyer to act for me.

- In 2018, my former lawyer, to whom I made an advance payment to represent me, told me I should get a different solicitor because he had changed his profession.

- My family back in Africa, especially my mother, who just turned 80 years old, requested I bring my children to her so that she can bless them as our culture demands. However, this was not possible because of the ongoing crisis with my ex-spouse.

- I am a civil infrastructure engineer; I want to inspire my children, help them gain from my university experience, and do more than I have achieved. However, this has not been possible because my ex-spouse has refused me from having contact with them.

- As a parent, I must let my children know my culture as a heritage. I believe this will give them some balance in their lives, allow them to be part of an extended family in Africa and Europe, help them build their character and enhance their lives. However, this has not been possible as my children have not been allowed to construct their identities and build a sense of pride around being part of a culture and heritage.

Mark has voluntarily provided this statement to support the purpose of this book. He has not relented in his efforts and continues to seek ways to contact his children. His name has been changed to protect his identity.

In the next chapter, I will share my story, and together, we will explore a to-do list you can tick to help you gain access to your children after a divorce. The process is less complicated than you think. All you need is the knowledge of the proper steps and a willingness to commit to the journey. The solution to any problem is always one step away.

CHAPTER TWO

YOU CAN HAVE ACCESS TO YOUR CHILDREN

I had been married to the mother of my children for over 7 years. All was going well; I had always thought we would spend the rest of our lives with each other, together with our children. I never saw a divorce or separation in our future. I knew how messy it could get for the entire family, and I never wanted that. But it happened.

For over two years, my ex-spouse and I struggled to get on the same page on different issues. It was like waking up from a dream—a dream you thought was perfect. That dream had been to get married, have my own children, and be a good role model in their development. It started off as I had wished—getting married and having children. All I was focused on was looking after my family and ensuring my children got the best of everything. I was ever-present in their lives and eventually built a well-deserved father-child relationship (the Attachment Bond). I was sure this would have a positive impact on their sense of self, development, growth, and future relationships with others. This was exactly what I had dreamed of.

However, at a time during the marriage, things started getting downhill, and unnecessary problems started creeping into our matrimonial home. My ex-spouse's behavior became unreasonable, and she started suspecting every move I made. Although this was unusual for me, I maintained my calm because I wanted peace in our home. The situation got worse and completely out of control, leading to several arguments and confrontations. This was a sign that the marriage was breaking down. We started maintaining our personal spaces and talking less to each other. As our communication started breaking, I knew the sanctity of our marriage was at stake. Trust became a thing of the past, and our marriage suffered for it. We managed to get some of our family friends involved to see if the problem could be solved. Their interventions, although well-intentioned, did not help, and we ended up separating and getting a divorce later.

Being away from my children was difficult, but it was a challenge I needed to get myself ready to tackle. I struggled to come to terms with the divorce, vowing never to be separated from my children. This is the part where I advise all parents never to give up on their children, even after a separation. In this case, it is the children's future that matters the most, and every responsible parent must stand strong, face the challenges, and do the right thing. Numerous studies have highlighted that some children raised in single-parent families are at heightened risk for depression, substance abuse, anxiety, externalizing behaviors and disorders, lower school achievement, more discipline problems, more crimes, and incarceration. Parents should, therefore, bear in mind the consequences of these highlighted outcomes and ensure they take center stage in the development of their children, even after a separation.

Although some children raised in single-parent families have become very successful in their later lives, it is generally beneficial for children to have both parents in their upbringing, as a secure attachment with both parent's, helps to promote the children's cognitive, emotional, and social development. It also helps the children exhibit positive social behaviors. It should be noted that the healthy involvement of both parents in their children's day-to-day lives helps ensure that their children can perform better socially and academically.

The situation at my home was becoming a nightmare, and I couldn't sleep. I was freaking out and kept wondering what to do. I would ask myself several questions, like, what if I am divorced and I can only see my children when a court approves it? What will my life be like without my children? Can I bear this situation, and if so, for how long? Will this not affect my mental health? If I continue this way, what will become of me? At this point, I was already underperforming at work. I had lost weight and the zeal to do anything remotely productive with myself. I withdrew myself and continued to wallow in my suffering.

I made up my mind to accept the situation and be strong for my children, no matter the outcome. On one of our bad days, things got out of hand, and the situation started to get violent. It was at that point that I decided that the best way for me to handle the issue was to leave my matrimonial home. Even before leaving, my ex-spouse created a scene, and I had to get the police involved. For the first time in my life, I was almost placed in custody for a crime I didn't commit. I, however, defended myself well, proved my innocence, and consequently freed myself from the false accusations.

After leaving my matrimonial home, my ex-spouse stopped me from seeing my children. It was her way of punishing me because she knew how much I loved my children and would love to spend time with them. To be honest, it was extremely difficult to accept. I never thought I would one day live away from my children, so I decided to seek legal advice and eventually made an application to the court for custody, as my ex-spouse was adamant that she would not allow me to see my children or have any contact with them. My application was granted, and I was finally given the right to have regular contact with my children.

After seeing my family split up, leaving my matrimonial home, being denied my children for a while, fighting to see them in the court of custody, and now regaining that access, I see it as a responsibility to help other parents who are going through similar situations. One of the things that helped me cope well was my ability to accept the situation first and then find positive and possible ways of dealing with it without getting the children directly involved. You must never forget that in this situation, the protagonists are the children.

Today, I tell a different story. I write from a place of victory—the same victory I want you to experience. In the next chapter, I'll walk you through some of the key steps I took to succeed in this journey.

CHAPTER THREE

THE STRATEGY YOU NEED TO GAIN ACCESS TO YOUR CHILDREN

Sometimes, happily ever after takes less time than you expected. When you love someone, you convince yourself that you're going to love them for the rest of your life. Unfortunately, things happen, and priorities change over time. Does marriage have to be this complicated? Who in the world would be excited to see the marriage they put so much work into split? Or who would like to separate from a family they hold dear?

One thing we must understand, though, is that divorces and separations happen. Marriages do not always end happily or when deaths do them apart. People make mistakes. There is distrust. Life throws curveballs that prove too strong for couples to handle. Regardless of the reason, it is difficult for both parties when a marriage ends.

When I met my ex-spouse, I thought the love we had for each other, the peace, and everything would never change. But it did. Even before the divorce became the only option, there was no more peace, and

I saw things gradually wither and become unbearable. At that moment, I left my matrimonial home, and my ex-spouse immediately stopped me from seeing my children. I got anxious and depressed. All I wanted was just one thing: to contribute to the upbringing of my children. I did not want to become a stranger to them. I wanted to show them how much I loved them as they grew up. I knew this was possible, even after a divorce. The question was, how?

I'm happy I was able to get out of the situation successfully. Maybe you've tried to get out of the situation, but you continue to fail. You've tried to sort things out, but it seems insurmountable. There is hope. If you're ready to reverse this situation, then check out the different strategies I implemented to help me achieve my goal. These same strategies have helped several other parents who are struggling to gain access to their children.

Take the first step.

To see change in any situation, you must first begin with yourself. It starts with you coming clean to yourself about the whole issue. Acknowledge your involvement and take responsibility. With that, you'd be able to strategize with a clear mind. You should also seek additional legal advice, as this is an important part of your divorce process, especially when children are involved. You could also try speaking to anyone close to your ex-spouse. Make sure every conversation is recorded. Even after the divorce, don't forget to record your exchanges so you can present them in court whenever it is needed or if the terms are breached. In chapter 4, we will dive deep into how to leverage legal advice for expected results.

Communicate with the primary parent of your child(ren)

It's often said that communication is the key to building a successful relationship. In the same way, an amicable divorce requires effective communication. However, what happens when communication is broken? When it's no longer possible to communicate without hostility and emotionally draining manipulation. In chapter 5, I'll walk you through the best ways to communicate your way to a harmonious divorce.

Seek legal advice.

A broken marriage could consume your entire life, leaving you clueless and directionless. With concerns about your children, finances, a separated family, uncertainties about the future, and dealing with heartbreak, it's almost impossible to catch a break. At this point, you'll need someone trusted to guide you through the process. This is where seeking legal advice comes in. In chapter 6, I will share with you how to seek legal advice in the right way and use it to your advantage.

Build a personal relationship with your child.

It is difficult to keep your children completely away during a divorce, but this is the time you should invest in building a stronger relationship with them. With everything going on, it is important not to lose contact with your children, even if you don't live under the same roof. I'd walk you through the step-by-step process I implemented to build an unbreakable personal relationship with my children. This will ensure you keep your children far away from the chaos.

Take care of yourself.

Whether it is during or after it is finalized, a separation is never easy to digest. Many people are unable to cope with such a drastic change and have lost it during these critical moments. Hence, it is important that you take proper care of yourself moving forward. Separation is one of the most draining things you will ever experience in your lifetime, and if you don't take care of your health, you may never recover from it. Although it was quite hard, I got up on my feet and learned to live my way. In chapter 9, I'll help you with the same strategies I implemented for my personal care.

Manage stress positively.

How do you manage distress during a separation? As you can imagine, there are many ways to manage distress. However, choosing to handle them well will positively affect every aspect of your life and your relationship with others. By prioritizing positive distress management, I was able to lead a peaceful life. In chapter 10, I will teach you exactly how to manage distress during this very challenging time.

Get external help.

Do you know how comforting it is to know someone is listening to you and empathizing with you? It is never easy, and many times, people might not even understand what you're going through unless they've experienced the same things. Therefore, it is important that, while going through a divorce or separation, you seek external help from the right people. This will help you make fewer mistakes that may worsen the situation. We'll address this in Chapter 10.

Adopt a coping strategy.

A separation from the people you love the most would emotionally affect even the strongest man in the world. Therefore, the question here will never be whether you will feel pain or not. It is how you will cope with the pain without letting it affect the rest of your life. By choosing a healthy coping strategy, you learn to tolerate and minimize the pain of the separation. In chapter 11, I'll share some of the coping strategies that helped me manage the pain of my divorce and separation from my children.

So, there you have it! The strategies I implemented to achieve my goals. These are the same strategies that have helped many other parents gain access to their children after their separation. Although it may not feel like it, you can still have a good and happy life after your divorce—a good and happy life where you remain a major influence in the upbringing of your children.

CHAPTER FOUR

TAKE THE FIRST STEP

Nothing is quite as unpredictable as love and marriage. No one signs a marriage certificate and looks forward to signing the divorce papers. Well, most people don't. It's even worse when your children are involved. This is the kind of situation that leaves you feeling completely clueless and even helpless. However, if you want to still make a good life for yourself and still be the best parent you can be despite the separation, you must take the first step.

- It won't be easy.
- It will be a nightmare.
- But it must be done.

It was a nightmare come true to leave my children behind. It was even worse when my ex-spouse refused me access to my children. I never thought a day like that would come, and I had sleepless nights thinking of what to do next. Soon enough, I discovered that the first step to solving my problems was getting the right information.

Getting legal advice and support

Like in most developed countries, the first step to dealing with a divorce is seeking legal advice and additional support. If both parents cannot agree on cordial arrangements for their children, a married or unmarried parent can obviously make an application to the court to be granted custody of their children. In the case where an unmarried parent does not have parental responsibility, they can still make an application to the court to get a parental responsibility order. It is important for every parent to be aware of this process. Nonetheless, the process is as grueling as every other court case, especially when the primary parent refuses to cooperate.

Following my divorce, the mother of my children withdrew my access to my children. Even after several attempts at negotiation, she was adamant that I would not see my children. Due to my desperation, I had to seek legal advice. I went to the court, and after a couple of hearings, I was eventually granted access to my children, which was the best outcome I was looking for.

My advice, therefore, is to keep hope alive even if negotiations with the primary parent do not work out well. As a parent, you have a responsibility toward your children and the right to see them. If you are refused that right, you can make it happen through supervised or unsupervised contacts. This is the power that the right information can give you. Overall, I advise that you stay calm, stay positive, and be proactive in any action you take. Contact the right people, seek the right help, and take the appropriate actions.

Speak with the primary parent.

Kicking off the conversation with the primary parent won't be easy, especially after the case is taken to court and settled. In every conversation with the primary parent, make sure you go straight to the point and tell them what you want. Agree on a meeting place outside both your homes for neutrality's sake, especially if the separation is messy. Finding common ground where no one is at an advantage will help the conversation flow well. Also, record your exchanges so you can present them to the court if needed.

The conversations I had with my ex-spouse about regaining access to my children were worse than I imagined, although I was not too surprised by her actions after living with her for so many years. She was at times abusive, intolerant, demanding, and controlling because she had full custody of the children and thought she was in total control of the situation. It was like hitting a brick wall, and there were zero signs of us ever reaching an agreement. She made the situation very difficult for me.

Accept the situation and remain calm.

It won't be easy to accept a situation where you are restricted from seeing your children. In fact, it'll be unbearable and devastating. But regardless of the situation, being agitated, violent, abusive, or threatening will not help your case. Therefore, the solution is to always remain calm, no matter how hard it gets. This is crucial to the entire process because it helps you fully concentrate and stay in control of everything that's happening. It will also help you abstain from certain actions you may take that you will regret later or forever.

There is a solution to every problem. Whatever the case may be and however difficult it gets, be reassured that there will be a positive outcome in the end if the right actions are taken. As I have mentioned throughout this book, following the right path will always lead you to success.

Keep a record of contacts and communication.

You can keep records of your communication through emails, text messages, or letters. This record will not be for you to publish online but will be relevant in court if needed. This way, you will not be breaching confidentiality and creating more legal problems for yourself. So, be discrete and keep records.

In one of the situations I was involved with, communication was a vital tool, and it worked well, so there was no need for the alienated parent to make an application to the court. When the couple separated, the primary parent of the children restricted the alienated parent from seeing the children. Since they were family friends, I decided to intervene. I had a clear conversation with the primary parent and explained how important it is to let the alienated parent have contact with their children. The primary parent saw reasons with me and finally agreed to let the alienated parent see their children. However, it was not easy to resolve the matter because the primary parent was beyond livid with the alienated parent due to their messy separation. When the primary parent finally calmed down and reflected on the issue, they realized that their decisions were borne out of anger and that keeping the children away from their other parent would affect them negatively in the long run. The matter was resolved amicably, and the alienated parent started having regular contact and spending quality time with their children. I pray that a lot of other parents can follow this example and be able to manage their emotions and anger so it does not get to the point where they continue to refuse access of the children to the other parents and force them to make applications to the courts, especially those parents who do not want to give up on their children, as I have demonstrated from my personal experience in this book.

While it is normal for parents to run to every Jack and Jill seeking counsel on how to best solve this issue, they may be discerning because different people will only give advice based on their own perspectives. They are quite vulnerable at this stage and prone to making rash and perhaps wrong decisions. However, I urge every parent to take several deep breaths, think of the future of their children, and only internalize positive counsel.

CHAPTER FIVE

COMMUNICATE WITH THE OTHE PARENT OF YOUR CHILD(REN)

You found yourself out of your home in the middle of a stormy night. You were confused. You looked up at the bright sky, where rain and snow mixed in a dramatic fashion. You tried to find the source of that tension between you and your spouse, yet you couldn't find it. After some time, you reach the understanding that there's nothing you can do about it. Now, you must get on with life, no matter how difficult the circumstances you're dealing with are. The relationship breaks down, the divorce papers are signed, and that is it. There is no marital union like before. You are back to strangers now, maintaining very little or no contact at all.

Communicating with the primary parent might have already been broken down before you got divorced. Now, after the divorce, there's even more that needs to be done. There is more to talk about and agree on! First, you would need to agree on how to raise your children going forward. You want to be co-parents together, so you need to make sure to co-parent properly, and one of the most difficult parts of transitioning back into co-parenting is communication after the divorce. During a divorce, communication within the marriage often degrades into a poor or non-existent state, and after the divorce is final, this trend will naturally worsen.

Since I have experienced this, I am in a position to give you some advice on how to work on communicating effectively with the primary parent of your children and through the right medium. This is what I would do in the subsequent paragraphs.

Try to initiate the communication.

Communicating with your ex-spouse after divorce comes naturally to no one, but if you want to ensure that your relationship with your children is as good as possible, it's critical that you work on it. Let me ask you a quick question: Do you remember what happened the last time you communicated with your ex-spouse? Were you on the same page, or did things just not go well at all?

For instance, communicating with my children's mother started with phone calls that I had to discontinue because of the tension she caused. My next step was to only communicate through emails and text messages to reduce the tensions.

Note that while doing this, you must stay cautious of the things you say and write. Don't forget that the other person might be recording all your conversations, waiting for the perfect time to use your own words against you. Therefore, it's important to always stay calm and be mindful of how you communicate. That calmness will place you in control of the situation and help you achieve your goal quicker.

After initiating contact with my ex-spouse, everything was going according to plan until her mood switched. She had her good days and days when she had no interest in any form of communicating with me. I went through some of our respectable family friends, and although she would agree to change her ways, she would, for no particular reason, become unbearable and unreasonable again just after one week of having positive conversations and solutions. At that point, I had no other option than to pursue the legal process because I was keen to have regular contact with my children.

In a nutshell, if you try to sustain communication with the primary parent of your children through calls, text messages, emails, or close and trusted relatives and yet nothing changes, then it is an indication that you need to go to court. By this time, you would have gathered enough evidence to win the case. The court might order you to go back and try to initiate a friendly arrangement. So, it is important to keep all the evidence you have gathered through your communication, as you can show the court that you have tried, but it did not work out well.

My children's mother would sometimes appear to be very willing to cooperate and would willingly agree to let me see my children. But a few days later, she would, for no reason, become unrecognizable and difficult to communicate with. She would be completely against me seeing the children and would stop our amicable arrangements. I think that she completely took advantage of the love I had for my children. She continued to demonstrate unreasonable behavior by stopping me from having contact with them. These were the challenges I faced, and I have come to realize that many other parents abandon their children because they cannot cope with the challenges of dealing with the primary parent.

Speak to close and trusted people.

There is a popular saying that it is only in your challenging seasons that you know who your true friends are. Seeing this as unarguably one of the most challenging seasons of your life, you must take a mental stock of your closest and most trusted friends and relatives and talk to them. If you have tried every possible means to initiate a conversation with the primary parent of your children and they still refuse to communicate with you, then try a trusted relative or friend. This can be a mutual friend, a sibling, or even another parent. Also, avoid bringing people you know would be biased in the judgment because this would frustrate the process for you. Even after involving trusted people, you may still want to put it in the back of your mind that you may not get the desired outcome. In my case, I reached out to some trusted and respectable friends, but it still led us to nowhere. I was lucky and able to benefit from positive advice and guidance from my brother, who is a Barrister. His input helped me a lot to deal appropriately with the situation and process. I felt more confident and assured each time I communicated with him. His advice was second to none and he made sure his words and actions were aligned with my goal.

Communication Channels

There is no one channel to communicate with a person you have just divorced. These are four of the most popular:

- Emails
- Text messages
- Letters
- Verbally

With mobile technology, sending emails and text messages can be done easily. However, in many cases, these channels can be ignored, and there is no way of confirming that they have been received. This is where posting letters could be useful. You write your letter, send it through the post office as registered and signed for mail, be rest assured that it will be received. This way, you can even track the letter. If they are willing to talk to you, they'll respond after receiving the letter. If they don't, you'll at least have confirmation that your letter was delivered successfully. No matter how hard the primary parent makes it for you or how much they hurt your feelings, never lose hope and never give up.

Divorce can be devastating, but it doesn't have to be. Nothing is going to be the same between you and your ex after the divorce is finalized, but if you put these tips I have provided into practice when communicating with your ex, you should be able to realize that things might get a little easier after the divorce.

The key thing to remember here is that it is your responsibility to develop a better relationship with the primary parent, as your children will benefit from it, and both of you will heal from the separation quicker, and there will be no bitterness or resentment between both of you at the end. You are both living your separate lives now, and your children will understand your decisions better when they are older.

Despite the challenges posed by the primary parent to ensure the alienated parent does not have access to their children, alienated parents should be aware that they have as much right to contact and care for their children as the primary parent. It is important to understand this legal provision and leverage it, as you will benefit from it when things start to go wrong.

CHAPTER SIX

SEEK LEGAL ADVICE

As explained in the previous chapter, if the arrangement between you and the primary parent does not work, then you need to seek legal advice. In fact, there are laws that give both parents equal rights in the custody of their children, but you wouldn't know if you didn't ask the right person.

There are many parents still fighting to be with their children, and there are also those who have been through the system but have experienced difficulties, as Mark clearly pointed out in his story. No matter what category you're in, you can use the strategies I used, which I have clearly mentioned in this book.

See a lawyer

If you are going to see a lawyer, you must be prepared to pay for their services and a court fee. These lawyers are trained professionals capable of giving you up-to-date legal advice, guidance, and support. Meeting them will help you understand the processes, procedures and protocol you must follow to have access to your children, as it is well within your rights to do so. But I'd tell you this: it is not the same in all countries. When it comes to choosing a solicitor, it's important for you to know and be able to distinguish the variety of existing specializations. Personal injury, family law, immigration, employment, wills and probate, and commercial are some of the most common specializations of solicitors. In this situation, you'd need a family law solicitor. This professional will also tell you how your case would work and how long it may take to resolve it.

If you don't want to go straight to the solicitor, then my advice is to first discuss it with someone who's in the legal profession, someone who can give you good advice. Even though you'd still need a lawyer, seeking the advice of a trusted friend in the legal profession will give you a good head start. However, make sure you're discreet when selecting and confiding in this person. You can always find information on the internet, but it is advisable to hear from the mouth of the law itself.

Apply for a court order.

After meeting with a solicitor, you'll be given some options. Some of the best solicitors will advise you to go to court, fill out the court form, pay your fees, and then it's done. And some others will offer to do all the work for you for a fee. But if the case is not that complicated and you have not been involved in problems that could tarnish your image, some solicitors would tell you to go straight to court and represent yourself. If you know there might be some complications with your case, then it is advisable to go to the solicitor; otherwise, you'll feel trapped in court.

One thing you should note here is that the court is open to everybody, and before the outbreak of COVID-19, it was possible to just walk up to the court reception, get a form, and go home to fill it out. At this point, you might still need to seek the help of a lawyer in answering some of the complicated questions, so you do not implicate yourself by providing the wrong answers. While some lawyers would tell you just what to do, others would charge you for their time and services. Upon completion of your form, you'd need to take it back to the reception desk of the court and wait for a hearing date. This is how I completed my process and got myself a hearing date. Please note that the process of making an application may have changed during the COVID-19 period as applications are completed online and cases are heard virtually. It is advisable to get the right information before starting an application.

Speak to Social Services

Speaking to a social service worker, the priority in every situation is the child's safety and wellbeing. Since your presence in your child's life is guaranteed to improve that, it is advisable to speak to Social Services and let them know exactly what is going on between you and the primary parent. Normally, the court will speak to Social Services to find out if they're aware of any concerns regarding your family. So, in case you have already reported the problem to them, it might obviously be in your favor if they are contacted by the court regarding their involvement. Therefore, it is advisable to make Social Services aware of the problems so that they can relate them to the court when the time is right.

Speak to the police.

Like social services, speaking to the police is a great way to make a case for yourself in court. This is because the court will also contact the police to find out if they've had any dealings with your family. However, if there have been queries or shouting at home, the police might have been alerted by your neighbors, and this might reflect badly on your case. If you're not too sure of what might happen, you could just let them know what is happening at the time. So, in case they're called up to the court, they'd say you've contacted them, and they are aware of the problem.

If there is anything that I hope you take away from this, it's to be there for your children. Even though your marriage doesn't work out despite the work and effort you put into it, you should still fight to be there for your children. Don't let any "what ifs" or regrets cloud what should be a bright future for you and your children. Try these steps, even when it is hard. At the end of the day, you and your children's wellbeing should always remain your number one priority. Hopefully, by going through these steps in the right order, you will be able to access your children and move on with your life peacefully.

CHAPTER SEVEN

BUILD A PERSONAL RELATIONSHIP WITH YOUR CHILD

By creating personal and secure relationships with your children, you teach them to regulate their emotions in stressful and difficult situations. This also helps with their mental and emotional development, boosting their self-confidence and overall sense of well-being. It is not a secret that good communication is an important aspect of building any good relationship. Therefore, you need to invest in good communication if you want to build a healthy and reliable relationship with your children. Do read further to understand how to overcome the communication challenges of separation and still maintain a healthy personal relationship with your children.

The easiest way to deal with this is to keep in mind that the children are in the middle of everything. Therefore, you must make it a priority to keep a healthy relationship with them without involving them in the process. You understand that anything that must get to your children must first go through the primary parent. If the primary parent is willing to communicate with you and reach a compromise, then it won't be so difficult. But if they refuse to make any contact with you on the matter and frustrate your efforts to spend time with your children, then you can go legal, as outlined in the previous chapters. Apart from those legal steps, you could also do the following things to maintain contact with your child (ren).

Get a phone for the child.

Even after obtaining legal custody, you may still not get the opportunity to communicate with your children every day. Arrangements are often agreed on a fortnightly basis. However, exceptions can be made based on your schedule. In that case, getting a phone for them will help you stay in touch. In most cases, even after buying a phone for your child and securing legal custody, the primary parent may still take the phone away from the child under the guise of protecting the child from distractions. Don't let that deter you. Keep trying. Also, you may have to negotiate with the primary parent to restore the children's access to their phone. If you worry that your child may be too young for a phone, then you should understand that desperate times call for desperate measures. There is no legal age for owning a mobile phone, and no legislation prevents you from getting one for your child. If the primary parent objects, you could reach a compromise with them to allow you to speak to the children through their phone. In my case, I gave my children phones when they were very young, and this helped me stay connected to them, although time and again, their mother would take the phones away from them, and I would not be able to communicate with them for a while. This was a process I had to get used to.

Whether you can get a phone for your child or not, you should be aware that most contact will have to go through the primary parent. You must either call or text them. In fact, the court would be pleased if it went through them. Some primary parents may even want all communication to go through them, and if they agree to you speaking to the child through their phone, they will be present to listen in. They can ensure that while they are present, you will have limited time to chat with the child, making it even more difficult for the child to speak freely. My advice is to keep the interactions with your child (ren) basic. Avoid engaging in delicate topics with them, as this may inspire the primary parent to frustrate your efforts even further. When the children are over at your home, you can talk to them about anything. Please avoid discussing negative aspects of the primary parent with them, as it is very easy to be drawn into these kinds of discussions. The children should be completely kept away from your problems.

To minimize the tensions between you and the primary parent while you are trying to get through to them, endeavor to stay calm and listen to them more. Don't interrupt them while they're talking, and try your best to be as agreeable as possible. While talking to your child (ren), listen patiently to what they're saying, whether you agree with it or not. Don't try to stop them from talking, even when you disagree. Simply listen and offer them the advice you desire. Also, avoid close-ended questions that require only yes or no answers. Ask them open-ended questions, giving room for more light and interesting conversations.

Stay strong for your child(ren).

Research has proven that thousands of alienated parents have given up on building a personal relationship with their children, especially after separation, because the primary parents have made it so difficult for them to have access to the children. Some of the alienated parents have consequently moved on with the mindset that the children will reach out to them when they are grown, have a voice of their own and can make their own decisions. However, this is totally wrong because although this has happened in some cases, not every child will reach out to their alienated parent who was not in their lives when the children needed them most.

The reason I stood firm for my children was because I never wanted them to grow up without having a secured attachment with me. But also without me contributing to their upbringing and development. I had a friend in London who was estranged from his father. They both knew each other and would pass by each other without anyone acknowledging the other. Unknown to them, they were biologically related, and it was father and son. It was sad because the father, who was denied access to his son by the mother, did not do much to maintain a relationship with his son, and we have just seen the sad outcome. So, even if you're going through a difficult time or the primary parent decides to make it difficult for you, I urge you not to give up. In order to stay strong and fight for access to your children, I advise you to engage in activities that will build up your resilience and find a community of people you can always rely on. This will help you keep up the hope, even when it seems lost.

If you give up, you may end up losing contact with your child and not knowing what he or she even looks like in the future. A Nigerian friend of mine had given up on trying to stay in contact with his son because his ex-spouse had made it so difficult for him to have access. He finally gave up and abandoned his son. The boy later became a professional football player and signed a major contract with a professional football club. Years later, his son had the courage to meet him. To his son's greatest surprise, he discovered that everything his mother had told him about his father was false. He found out that throughout the separation, his father had tried everything to be a part of the family and support his development but later gave up because his mother was so difficult to deal with and had refused any contact with his father. Despite their reunion, the father had ultimately missed out on some of the most important moments in his son's life and development, which he still regrets not being able to contribute to.

Years ago, whilst on my school placement, I had a chat with a young Occupational Therapist (OT). He told me that when he was a little boy, his mother (primary parent) told him a lot of stories about how his father was a wicked man and didn't want to support his upbringing. He told me that when he grew up, he met his father online and realized everything his mother had told him about his father were lies. After that revelation, he said to me, “Michael, I didn’t love my mother; I don't think I'll ever talk to her again.” Every day, one parent lies to a child somewhere in order to tarnish the reputation of the other parent (parental alienation). Some children grow up to discover the lies. Some don’t. Whichever happens, it is still dishonorable for one parent to say despicable things about the other parent because there is a good chance that the child will find out someday, somehow. This is also not good for a child’s development. Unlike the therapist I mentioned above, the child may breed animosity toward that parent and grow up feeling unloved and even hot-tempered, affecting their character and even their performance in school.

This is my best practice for building a healthy personal relationship with one’s child after a separation. Seeing your children once a month will not build the rapport they need to understand and acknowledge your presence in their lives. Making an effort to always be available and present when you are (and even when you are not) needed will create a sense of security in the child’s subconscious mind. This is guaranteed to help you bond with your children better.

In chapter thirteen, I’ll explain what parental alienation is and its devastating effects on children and alienated parents.

CHAPTER EIGHT

SEEK MEDIATION/COUNSELLING

When I left my matrimonial home, I realized things were happening too fast, and my thoughts were all over the place. I had to continuously remind myself to take regular deep breaths and give myself time to adjust to the change. I consciously gave myself time to grieve so I could come to terms with the situation. I was deliberate about seeking help because I was desperate to maintain contact with my children. Doing that helped me overcome the difficult moments and challenges.

Below are a few ways to find common ground with your ex-spouse and reconnect with your children:

Seek Mediation.

Mediation and counseling are two distinct practices that are used to help individuals and groups resolve conflicts and address emotional or psychological issues. While there are similarities between the two practices, there are also significant differences in terms of their purpose, parties involved, confidentiality, desired outcome, timeframe, role of the mediator/counselor, legal status, training, and scope of practice. Understanding these differences is essential to choosing the most appropriate process for resolving a specific problem or issue. However, this book is about resolving the child custody problem between the primary parent and the alienated parent.

Although many issues in a divorce or separation can be contentious, child custody and parenting time are often the most emotionally charged and difficult for parents to agree on. Mediation is intended to help tone down the hostility for the sake of both parents and their children. It helps the parents negotiate a mutually acceptable agreement regarding the custody of the children where the mediator will support the parents in making their own decisions, as no decision will be imposed on them by the mediator. Mediation can be either ordered by a court or private and voluntary. Mediation in child custody is typically more cost-effective than going to court because you are paying one mediator to help you come to an agreement with the other parent, rather than both of you paying hourly fees to separate mediators. Also, you are given the opportunity to have a say in the mediation sessions, which is a luxury that is practically non-existent in the court process. It is vitally important to remember that child custody, in general, and mediation, in particular, are not primary between you and the other parent. It is about the children. So, you have to make a commitment to do whatever is best for your children, and that starts with you being prepared to attend mediation sessions and make a positive contribution.

Seek Counselling

Dissimilar to mediation, counseling involves you working collaboratively with a counselor and delving into underlying issues that drive unproductive behaviors, helping you to build healthy coping skills and getting more of what you want out of life. It is obvious that when you have been denied access to your children, especially when you have built a secure attachment and rapport with them, you will be negatively affected in one way or the other. For example, you may be struggling with anxious thoughts or a depressed mood. You may feel stuck in your head and ruminate about not seeing your children or having any form of contact with them. You may equally feel that your world has come to an end. This is when counseling can help you regain awareness of the present and help you focus on the present moment, making you more effective in your daily life. Counseling can help you develop skills to cope more effectively with stressful situations. Rather than merely reacting to situations, counseling can help you gain the skills to move forward productively. In addition, counseling can give you the ability to take a step back and re-evaluate how you can respond to the situation with the other parent regarding your children. Although counseling has several benefits, its primary purpose is to help you achieve more of what you want to achieve. It helps you gain insight into ineffective behavior patterns, unhelpful thoughts, and unproductive ways of coping with painful emotions.

Talk to a trusted friend or relative.

Even though it doesn't directly solve your problems, talking to someone you trust can ease some of the tension you have built up. It is often said that a problem shared is a problem half solved, and that's true, especially when you share the problem with the right person. The right person, in this case, would be someone who would not use your problems against you for any reason. I personally advise that you always go with your instincts. This way, if it doesn't work the way you thought, you will be willing to take responsibility for your mistakes. This is unlike when your actions are externally influenced and you have someone to blame.

Contact the child's school.

In most circumstances, this is less important because, after the separation, you might no longer have the right to pick up your child from school if the primary parent has informed the school that you have left the matrimonial home and do not have access to the children. Regardless, informing the school of what has occurred is appropriate. You can communicate with the head teacher, letting them know that if they don't see you for a while, it's just because of what's going on. The headteacher can then relay your message to the children's class teacher. You should do this to avoid any complications should an emergency arise. I recall going to check on my son following an incident that had occurred at the school, but I was not allowed to see him. It was only after insisting and telling the head teacher that I have parental responsibility for my son that she finally allowed me to see him. I was made aware that his mother had instructed the school not to allow me to see him. The headteacher later apologized on this occasion after realizing that I knew my parental rights. This also helped me to keep track of what was going on in school with my children.

CHAPTER NINE

PERSONAL Care

Divorce is not an easy process, and following it, you will be confronted with a variety of tough situations. This is why you must make personal care a priority. Although time does indeed heal most wounds, proper personal care will speed up the physical and mental process. If you let the separation consume you, it might have serious consequences for your health. Many people who are unable to cope with the disappointment eventually turn to substances guaranteed to give them a reprieve. My experience as a social worker taught me that this was not the best course of action. The best choice is to stay strong and avoid developing a harmful habit.

This is also one of the reasons why I wrote this book; as a social worker with many years of training and experience in assisting others, I was able to avoid getting into that situation. I've been there as well. I understand the anguish that comes with a divorce. Because of this, I understand how to control stress and not let it take over my well-being.

This chapter will help you with the necessary steps you can take to heal after such a significant change.

Don't Drink

It is very easy to develop a bad drinking habit while trying to drown the sorrows of a separation. This is even worse when you are also separated from your children. Since personal care is largely concerned with the preservation of your growth, you must make concerted efforts to avoid falling into a drinking pattern. This way, you can continue fighting for access to your child with a sane, sober mind. My recommendation to anyone who has become addicted to alcohol is to get therapy and be serious about their goals. There are numerous agencies and personal counselors available to help people get out of drinking and any other harmful habit they may be entangled with.

Spend time with trusted friends.

You can have as many friends as you want, but never forget who your trusted friends are. In case you are not sure who to trust, look back on the time you had a challenge and remember who was the most helpful to you then. Who was discreet with the information you shared with them, and who covered your back? You can rely on your instinct as well. When you decide who those friends are, have a chat with them about your issues and listen to their advice. Even then, be sensitive to the information you receive. Do not allow your decisions to be a complete reflection of the conversations you've had with these friends. Instead, let it be an internal conviction. Since you never really know who to trust, you can stick to sharing only 70% of your personal issues with them and keeping the rest to yourself.

Manage stress positively.

Severe health issues can easily materialize from being separated from your entire family. From high blood pressure to sadness, anxiety, and even addictive behavior, the list is endless. Therefore, knowing how to manage distress after divorce is so vital because it may have a wide-ranging impact on your life if you don't learn how to control it on time.

You can do the following to ease the tension and deal with stress:

- When stressed or anxious, take deep breaths.
- Avoid spending time alone.
- Seek counseling.
- Take several short walks.
- Go on a vacation.
- Avoid situations that would trigger you.
- Do not withdraw yourself from the company.
- Participate in regular sports.
- Eat well.
- Sleep well.
- Take time off work.
- Stay positive, even when it gets tough.
- Avoid speaking to your child's mother if she remains unreasonable.
- Avoid sharing your problems with unreasonable and insensitive people.

The important thing to keep in mind in this situation is that taking care of yourself may not be the first thing that crosses your mind after your separation, but you must prioritize it. Even though you might become impatient with a backlog of court dates and other obligations, it's crucial that you keep control over the problems that affect you and how you handle them.

CHAPTER TEN

GET EXTERNAL HELP

If you don't have the strength to fight for yourself and your children, you can seek help from those who have been in your situation before. For instance, support groups and counselors can be of great help. The internet is also a fantastic source of knowledge and assistance. There are many people who have been in your situation before, and they may be able to point you in the right direction as it relates to your issue. However, keep in mind that your goal is to get back on your feet and start a new life. You may be wondering, "How do I go about it?" This is exactly what I will show you in this chapter.

Search the Internet

The internet is a detailed compendium of some of the best information you can get anywhere. You can easily find thousands of search results for whatever you need help with. However, after conducting the search, make sure you narrow it down to the most relevant so you do not become confused about the next steps. Google and YouTube are two search engines I wholeheartedly recommend. You must, however, understand that while social media is beneficial, it also has drawbacks. So, be sure to filter only what is required of you and focus on only positive, actionable information.

Speak to Your Good Neighbors

Divorce is an isolating and emotionally demanding experience. You can acquire some control over the process and make it less painful by seeking help from others and gathering information. Your good neighbors, for example, can be of great help. However, take extra caution because not all neighbors care about you. If you have neighbors who would alert the police whenever they hear a raised voice on your property, then you probably shouldn't be talking to them about your marital problems.

Speak to your manager at work.

This depends largely on the nature of your job and your workplace culture. The emotional pressure from this situation may make you underperform at work, and you might need to take some time off. But you can't do that if your manager does not know what is going on, and you cannot simply cease working and expect to get paid. You'll get sanctioned or even fired. Even if you don't want to tell them everything, tell them what you're going through and that you need some time off. Also, your manager may even be able to assist you, depending on your existing professional relationship. Your manager may be able to refer or signpost you to the organization's support department. You must, however, be discrete and ensure that you're speaking with only the right people.

Work with a coach.

Many people are judgmental and cynical about the divorce process, making it difficult to find someone to talk to and gain support from. It may be easier to get through the experience and feel less alone if you receive assistance from others, and that is why many people hire divorce coaches.

You'll have to deal with lawyers and other professionals who aren't going to be of much help. So, you will need someone who can guide you through the process and help you become a better person after the divorce. Coaches like myself are here to help make that happen. However, you should exercise precautions, as there are many fraudulent coaches online. Also, choose someone who is familiar with the laws and institutions.

Your divorce is your chance at a fresh start. Therefore, remain strong for yourself and your children. Evaluate what you want out of life after the divorce, devise a strategy for achieving those goals, and then execute them. You'll be better for it.

CHAPTER ELEVEN

ADOPT A COPING STRATEGY

When it comes to coping tactics, there are numerous options guaranteed to help you go through your divorce feeling confident and ready to face the challenges that lie ahead. I used to research coping tactics online, seeing how others dealt with the circumstances and what strategies they found incredibly helpful at the time. But before you dive into a coping strategy, make sure you have taken the bold step of accepting the reality of your situation.

Personal Development

I found reading books and listening to motivational content to be beneficial. This is because the more you know about the issue, the better prepared you will be. I eventually learned that some facts must be accepted—facts like not sleeping under the same roof as your child or visiting them every day. It was a painful truth, but I learned to accept it. That was the turning point for me.

Also, I found that playing football and working helped me ease stress and even boost my mental performance. You don't want to lie in bed when you feel distressed all day. Your capacity for creativity in coming up with activities that can keep you motivated and give you more reasons to push forward will determine your ability to overcome every obstacle. I also recommend listening to soul-lifting messages, especially when you go on long walks. If you are an indoor person, always make sure that you listen to teachings that help you build inner strength. Studying the Bible is my first recommended strategy because the power in God's word has the ability to heal, comfort, and restore any broken heart.

Watching Relevant TV Programs

We used to watch on BBC 2 "We Are Family," a documentary series looking at complicated family relationships. They would invite family members and have them talk about certain issues that were of great benefit to the targeted audience. By being exposed to other people's perspectives on the same challenge I had, I was able to understand mine better.

Financial Sustenance

If you need to use the court, you must pay the court application fees. Also, if you have left your home, you will need money to purchase or rent a new property. You'll need money to pay for your new home, rent, and a deposit. This is a significant sum of money to be spent. Some people may not want to do that; they may prefer to remain in the scenario because they lack the financial resources to leave their house and start all over again. People should be aware of their financial status and what they have and ensure that they can handle the procedure. I was still a student when I divorced my wife, but I was working and able to survive. Therefore, make sure you have a steady stream of income to sustain yourself and even take yourself for treats.

It's not a secret that I learned a lot from my ex-wife, and now, from various successful relationships, I have learned that being with the same person for years is a trap. Sometimes, we are just too afraid to get out of the box. I had always thought that the most important thing for families was to be together through good and bad times. But life and happiness, I have discovered, are more than just family status.

CHAPTER TWELVE

FOLLOWING YOUR REUNION

The fight for your child(ren) is guaranteed to take its toll on you, especially if your ex-spouse proves to be even more unreasonable than you expected. However, rest assured that if you follow due process, especially as it relates to the systems in your state, region or country, you will be reunited with your children in no time. When that does happen, it is important that you work harder than ever before to be the parent your children need.

It is completely normal for children to remain attached to both parents, no matter what the circumstances are. So, it is important that you do not alienate your child. Reassure them that there will be continuity of care and support and that the separation will not affect their ability to provide for their vital material and emotional needs. Making this happen may sometimes result in unpleasantness and tension between you and your ex-spouse, but don't let that deter you from doing what is right for your child.

Never involve your child(ren) in serious, negative conversations. Never vent to them or try to make them understand your perspective. If you do this, chances are that you will build animosity toward the other parent in them. Be sure to separate your feelings from your behavior. No matter how angry or hurt you are, do not allow those feelings to dictate how you treat your child.

Finally, for the sake of your children and their overall well-being, work on improving your communication with your ex-spouse. The success of your new co-parenting endeavor rests on how cooperative and agreeable you both are. Anything less than that will not only affect you both but also spill over to the child(ren). Always ask yourself how your actions (or even words) will affect your child(ren), and let your answer guide your dealings with your ex-spouse. There is hope at the end of the tunnel.

The next chapter will look extensively at what parental alienation is, the devastating effects it has on targeted parents and children, and appropriate ways of protecting them from its lasting psychological consequences.

CHAPTER THIRTEEN

PARENTAL ALIENATION

In Chapter 3, I described how building a personal relationship with your children is important. However, it is unwise to build your own personal relationship with your children and destroy their relationship with the other parent. In Chapter 7, I briefly mentioned how some primary parents have said despicable things to their children about the other parents in order to tarnish their relationship with those targeted parents.

Based on research, over 22 million parents have been targets of parental alienation in the United States and other countries. It is estimated that 10 million parents have experienced what they perceive to be severe alienation from their children. Even so, the clinical problem of parental alienation has been underreported and underappreciated by the public at large. I believe it is a silent epidemic that must be acknowledged, and appropriate measures can be taken to eradicate it to save children and targeted parents from its devastating effects.

Parental alienation occurs when one parent turns the child against the other parent through manipulation, threats, or lies. The parent intentionally does so in order to damage the relationship between the child and the other parent and to limit their time with the child indefinitely. The child can believe anything that the primary parent said against the targeted parent, and vice versa, without the child having much understanding about the accusations. The child will obviously become the victim of both parents, as their sole aim is to tarnish each other's trust in order to gain the child's trust, as the child can believe whatever is said against the targeted parent, and vice versa. It is important to note that, for parental alienation to occur, one parent will choose to act cruelly and heartlessly toward the other parent. The alienating parent tends to value their interests over the child's well-being and will do everything to win against or punish the targeted parent, even when the outcome is detrimental to the child's well-being or interest, to say the least.

This can be detrimental to the child because it can cause low self-esteem, emotional distress, and damaged relationships for the child and the targeted parent. The child can develop unusual behaviors, such as rejection, hostility, disrespect, and cruelty, and can be extremely negative toward the targeted parent for unjustified and often untrue reasons.

Research has suggested that alienated children and parents suffer many negative outcomes, which can include psychological disorders such as anxiety, substance misuse, and depression. It may also lead to active suicidal ideation, and in some cases, targeted parents may eventually end up committing suicide. Furthermore, there have been reports of a decline in academic performance among children and decreases in the work productivity of targeted parents.

Research has further proven that parental alienation often occurs in very tense and volatile separations or divorces, particularly when there are bitter child custody battles. This behavior also often occurs if, upon separation, one parent cannot let the relationship go or they have remarried and may want to start over and erase the other parent by destroying their relationship with their children.

During my work with children in their adolescence and young adulthood ages, they reported a multitude of alienating behaviors that damaged their relationship with the targeted parents and how their own well-being was affected. Some of the children felt they were abused by their primary parents. According to them, their primary parents had complete control over their lives, as the children believed they did not have voices of their own. The children felt they were made to feel fear or guilt when they did not comply with the primary parents' view of the targeted parents. Some reported denigration of the targeted parents to the point where it completely damaged their bond with the other parents and destroyed their thoughts, memories, and emotions regarding the targeted parents.

I believe that greater public attention is needed to resolve this problem and protect children and families from the lasting psychological consequences for everyone involved. Society should continue to recognize the prevalence of parental alienation and its negative impact on families. It is, therefore, crucial to explore effective methods to combat this problem and foster healthy relationships within families.

Understanding and addressing parental alienation requires a comprehensive approach that includes educating parents on the devastating impact on families, focusing on the children's best interests, and seeking professional help when necessary. By addressing the underlying issues that contribute to parental alienation, parents can work toward repairing damaged relationships and promoting the well-being of their children.

Targeted parents often face overwhelming emotions and challenges when dealing with parental alienation. Developing healthy coping strategies to promote healing and maintaining a strong connection with their children is crucial. Parents can overcome alienation by consistently expressing love for the affected children. This reassurance helps to strengthen the bond between the targeted parent and their child. Genuine affection and emotional support can mitigate the negative influence of an alienating parent. Active listening from the targeted parent is crucial in understanding the child's feelings and experiences, and they should remain open and non-judgmental, allowing their children to share their thoughts and emotions freely. Targeted parents should also demonstrate empathy and patience to help create a safe space for open communication with their children.

Advice to targeted parents: Engaging in self-care practices and finding a support network can contribute to an improved sense of self-worth. This may involve seeking professional counseling, joining a support group, or engaging in physical and mental wellness activities.

Overall, the emotional well-being of the targeted parent is crucial to combating parental alienation. By nurturing a healthy self-image and maintaining open communication with their children, targeted parents can foster the resilience needed to overcome this challenging situation.

Conclusion:

Parental alienation is a form of psychological abuse that occurs when one parent, the alienating parent, manipulates a child's emotions to turn them against the other parent (the targeted parent). This manipulation often involves making false or exaggerated claims about the targeted parent to create a wedge between them and the child.

The targeted parent experiences significant emotional trauma as they struggle to maintain a healthy relationship with their child. This, in turn, harms the child, who is manipulated into believing that the targeted parent is abusive or dangerous, which further exacerbates the problem and damages the parent-child relationship.

Certain factors make some parents more susceptible to becoming alienators, such as a prevalence of selfishness, where they exhibit extreme self-centeredness and a lack of empathy for both their child and the targeted parent. This further compound the emotional impact on all parties involved.

It is important to recognize the warning signs of parental alienation and take steps to prevent or mitigate its harmful effects. Early intervention strategies include open communication with the child, seeking professional help, and, in severe cases, pursuing legal action to protect the child's best interests.

Overall, understanding parental alienation and its underlying factors is crucial for professionals and family members to support the targeted parent and the child and work toward building healthier and more stable family dynamics.

In the next chapter, I will walk you through ways of overcoming parental alienation and a case of false allegation.

CHAPTER FOURTEEN

OVERCOMING PARENTAL ALIENATION AND FALSE ALLEGATIONS

Even when a divorce is amicable, it is a situation that can be turbulent, and when children are involved, they often pay the price. One way this is manifested is through false allegations of abuse in child custody cases in order to gain full custody of the child. Typically, one parent accuses the other parent of physical and/or sexual abuse of their child to gain leverage in their court proceeding. This tactic can be particularly impactful because judges tend to award primary physical custody to the parent who made the allegation, even if the accused parent's actions are not substantiated. Thus, false allegations can be a powerful weapon to limit or deny custody and/or visitation in a hurtful manner. Generally speaking, false allegations of abuse are a form of parental alienation, as I will explain in this chapter. Nothing can be worse than a custody decision that is based on a false allegation. To make matters worse, once a custody allegation has been issued, modification of it is a burdensome and uphill challenge, as you will find out from my work with a parent who lost custody of her child because she was falsely accused of abuse by her ex-husband.

The case of Mrs. Regina Caeli (name changed to protect identity) was allocated to me. Mrs. Caeli is a 40-year-old female who lost legal custody of her child because of allegations made against her by her ex-husband. Although a strong instinctive reaction to an abuse allegation is expected, it can sometimes be counterproductive as a rushed response can make the situation worse, or a wrong decision is often taken to ensure the child is safe. In this case, full custody was immediately granted to the father who made the allegation, which I considered a rushed decision. In these situations, my belief is that a thorough assessment or investigation of the allegation is carried out before a decision is made. However, a rushed decision is always made for the protection and safety of the children. In other countries, however, this may be different in the sense that the child may be handed over to Foster parent(s). At the same time, the investigation is ongoing in order to separate the child from both parents. As a professional, I fully agree.

My work with Mrs. Caeli was aimed at determining if an allegation of abuse had occurred or not or whether the allegation was fabricated by the other parent making the allegation with the intent of sabotaging and harming Mrs. Caeli's relationship with her child and/or helping the court make a rushed decision to grant him full custody of the child. I also had to provide psychological support to Mrs. Caeli to help her maintain a healthy well-being. I ensured that Mrs. Caeli and her child, a 10-year-old boy, were part of my work. I wanted my conclusions and recommendations to be based on full and accurate information by fully involving them in the process. I did not contact the accusing parent, as my work was to provide professional support to Mrs. Caeli and her child and to establish if the allegations were genuine. One of the things I looked at was the timeline of when the allegation was reported. I noted that the allegation was reported during the child custody process and not before. I equally noticed that it was the first allegation of abuse reported against Mrs. Caeli, and it was reported during the custody process. During my work with Mrs. Caeli, I established that she does not have a history of abusing her child, and the first allegation was made after the custody process had started. At that point, I felt that the validity of the allegation must be questioned. Furthermore, I thought there might be a significant probability that the allegation was false. Mrs. Caeli's mental well-being was greatly impacted as a result of the false allegations and the immediate alienation from her child. She was clearly suffering from emotional distress and reported experiencing active suicidal ideation. She told me, "Michael, I do not have any reason to live without my child; my life is completely worthless." It was clear to me that the trigger for Mrs. Caeli's presentation was the loss of contact with her child. Although I provided her with some coping skills, such as cognitive restructuring techniques, I ensured I addressed the allegations and loss of contact with her child. I told Mrs. Caeli I was going to do my best to prove her innocence and reunite her with her child. However, I further explained that the judge would have the final decision to make. As professionals, we should be aware of passing the right information to the people we support and not giving them full assurances or complete hope when we do not know what the actual outcome will be. This can increase their anxiety if, in the end, they do not get the outcome they were expecting.

My work with Mrs. Caeli was also to establish the consequences of being alienated from her child and to identify appropriate coping strategies to deal with the situation. It was also to establish if the allegations were true or false and how she could be reunited with her child if the allegations were proven to be false. Although it appeared to be an uphill challenge, it was one I was looking forward to, as my aim was to ensure that Mrs. Caeli was reunited with her child, prove her innocence, and help her regain her sanity. Mrs. Caeli was experiencing significant trauma, anger, guilt, disconnect, and low self-esteem as she struggled to accept the allegations and the reality of losing contact with her child. It was also damaging to the child, who was manipulated into believing that his mother was abusive or dangerous to him, which is a means of damaging his relationship with his mother.

Mrs. Caeli vehemently denied the allegations when I interviewed her. She told me how she loves her child and wouldn't harm him. She expressed her desire to see her child and urged me to thoroughly investigate the allegations so I could prove her innocence, as she wanted her innocence proven so she could have her child back. I interviewed Mrs. Caeli's family members, some neighbors, and close friends as part of my investigation. Everyone was made aware of my recordings of the interviews. I sought their consent and made them aware I would be presenting the recordings to the court during the legal custody hearing. Every person I interviewed told me they had never seen Mrs. Caeli abuse her child. Instead, they reported the care and unconditional motherly love Mrs. Caeli has demonstrated toward her child.

I was granted permission by the court to interview Mrs. Caeli's child. Interviewing a minor is different from interviewing an adult. I considered the fact that the child might be experiencing traumatic distress regarding the problem between his parents. I had to be flexible considering his age. I went into the interview with a plan of areas I intended to cover during the interview. I encouraged the child to speak freely, asked open-ended questions, slowed down my rate of speech, allowed him to process my questions, and allowed him time to respond without interrupting him. I ensured I used the attending behavior communication skills to carry out this interview. Attending behavior is communicating through four components: the use of body language, vocal qualities, eye contact, and verbal tracking. This was an important communication tool to help me carry out a successful interview with the child. I also had to be mindful of cultural differences and how they could contribute to a successful outcome.

Statement from the child below:

"After my mom and dad separated, I spent a lot of time with my mom and spent some weekends with my dad at his house. Every time I was with my dad, he never stopped telling me that my mom was a bad person and was abusing me. Even though I did not believe what my dad was saying, there was nothing I could do. I decided not to tell my mom because I did not want to create any further problems between her and my father. I am happy that I have this opportunity now to make my voice heard. My mother loves me and has never abused me. I love my mother and want to spend time with her. I also love my father."

The child appeared to settle well in the interview and provided a massive statement and views. I was happy that the court granted my request to interview the child to get his views and wishes. As I did with the others, I ensured the child was aware of my recordings and that I was going to share his statement, views, and wishes with the judge. He agreed. The child appears to have suffered emotional instability, as his presentation indicated during the interview. The child reported low self-confidence and self-esteem and decreased academic performance. He told me he was struggling to concentrate on his day-to-day activities due to what his father told him about his mother. He was thankful that the matter was being investigated and wished for a proportionate outcome.

One of the important aspects of working with a family, especially when children are involved, is making sure their voices are heard and decisions are taken based on their best interests. This is sometimes an oversight for some professionals. I made sure that the child was seen by a psychologist, and he told the psychologist the same story. The psychologist's report was also included in my findings.

The judge carefully examined my reports, recordings, and findings presented to him during the hearing process. I also presented a police report, which I had requested during my investigation. The report stated that Mrs. Caeli had no recorded record of abuse on the police database. This report was significant as it played a vital role in the judge's verdict. The accusing father did not present any evidence to back up his allegations. Therefore, his accusations were considered unsubstantiated by the judge. After hearing both parties and careful consideration, the judge declared a proportionate outcome, which I, Mrs. Caeli, and her child were satisfied with. The judge said he was satisfied with the evidence and findings presented to him and decided that Mrs. Caeli should regain full legal custody of her child. The judge also granted visitation rights to the father. However, he added that the father would be fined for raising false allegations in order to tarnish the child's relationship with his mother and gain full custody of the child.

I played an active role in supporting Mrs. Caeli through my professional support and ensuring that a proportionate decision was reached. Above all, the key to engaging alienated parents is to validate their parental identity, combined with professional efforts focused on enhancing their role as active and responsible parents in a bid to advance the cause of co-parenting. This is exactly what I did.

I believe that an active program of outreach is essential, as alienated parents suffer from a lack of effective support services and remain a highly vulnerable population. Service providers need to be persistent and proactive, as it takes time to build and sustain engagement in the context of these parents' feelings of isolation, helplessness, and their tendency to wait until there is a crisis before accessing support. For example, Mrs. Caeli was highly involved with and attached to her child and was forcefully removed from her child's life, consequently resulting in her experiencing crises such as profound mental and psychological pain and active suicidal ideation.

Generally speaking, on the matter of parental alienation, I have come to realize that the problem is systemic in nature; that is, the problem lies primarily in the adversarial nature of the legal determination of parenting after divorce when children are involved. Parents are ultimately set up to fight in an effort to win primary custody of their children, and the system tends to reward those skilled in adversarial combat. Parents often win their case by disparaging the other parent as a parent, in effect engaging in alienating behaviors, and the system thereby encourages and produces alienating behavior. For example, BB's child was immediately removed from her care, and full custody was granted to her ex husband after he reported an allegation of abuse. This decision was taken without a proportionate investigation. A legal presumption of co-parenting to counter established cases of child abuse and family violence may, in fact, be the most effective means of combating parental alienation and curtailing its damaging consequences while at the same time protecting the safety and well-being of children at risk of alienating parents. The case of Mrs. Caeli is an example. My work with Mrs. Caeli was based on combating alienation and seeking to reunite her with her child while addressing the significant clinical challenges of working with her as an alienating parent suffering from emotional distress.

Key points to take away:

- Making sure decisions are taken in the child's best interest.
- Targeted parents experience distress as a genuine response to their predicament, which can be perpetuated by negative automatic thoughts. For example, targeted parents are experiencing suicidal ideation, as seen in Mrs. Caeli's case.
- Professionals need to assess suicidal risk when working with targeted parents and children.
- Targeted parents can benefit from coping skills, including restructuring techniques.
- Targeted parents to reunite with their children, as in Mrs. Caeli's case.
- Parental alienation is damaging to children and parents.
- Children exposed to these dysfunctional relational dynamics may manifest consequences in the medium, short, or long term.

- Parental alienation is a silent epidemic that must be acknowledged, and appropriate support must be provided to targeted parents and children.

CHAPTER FIFTEEN
CONCLUSION

Why I Wrote This Book

Partnerships and marriages create great familial bonds. Therefore, it is not a surprise that it can be quite devastating when those bonds are broken, even in situations where separation or divorce is expected. Everybody experiences pain and loss, even the children.

Despite the challenge, it is a period where both parents will have to make many practical decisions. It is expected that going forward, any decision must be for the good of innocent and vulnerable children. However, from my personal experience, children have endured terrible times following a separation because one parent has used them as weapons of warfare against the other parent. Although the reason for the separation may not completely lie with the parent, the primary parent chose to restrict access to their children as a form of punishment. In many countries, the law even supports this. In most countries, mothers are granted full custody of the children, while fathers are granted only visitation rights after the separation. In cases where the mother is unfit to have full custody due to considerations, full custody may be given to the father, or the children may be taken into Foster Care. Coupled with the emotional stress of coping with a separation and being unable to see their children, many parents have been forced to abandon all their efforts to reconnect with their families. It is for parents like these that I wrote this book. Parents who have been locked away from their children's lives and do not know where to start

The mother of my children fought very hard to refuse me access to my children after we separated because she blamed me for it. It was difficult for me to accept the fact that I would not be able to see my children. Instead of moping about, I contacted the right people and got the advice I needed to make the right decisions. In the end, I was granted access to my children by the court, and today, I am a very proud father who has contributed immensely to the development of my children.

I am therefore urging all parents not to give up and abandon their children. By reading this book, you will discover that there is a way to regain access to your child. If you need any help making that happen, I'd be happy to help you, just like I have helped many others. My contact details are provided in this book.

The involvement of both parents in a child's development is non-negotiable because it builds smart, confident, and outspoken children ready to contribute positively to their different communities. Leaving the raising to one parent will not help the child, and that is why this book is important, as it encourages divorced parents to work hard at reconnecting with their children, regardless of the problems and frustrations.

Key Points To Take Away From The Chapters

Take the First Step: Taking the right first step will guarantee that only the desired outcome is achieved in the end.

Communication: Effective communication is the best tool for building understanding and trust, especially with the primary parent of the children. Also, when seeking help and legal advice, effective communication plays a great role in helping you get your message across appropriately.

Getting the Right Advice: Depending on the reason for the separation or divorce, it could either get friendly or messy. It is a crucial time for both parents and the children. When one parent has been denied access to the children, knowing how and where to seek the right support is important. Some of those channels are trusted friends, the legal team, the police, and the Social Services Department.

Build a Personal Relationship with Your Children: Maintaining a personal relationship with your children and staying involved in their development is one of the best decisions to take. As I have already mentioned in this book, staying involved in your children's upbringing and development improves their self-esteem, helps them adjust to the situation, and helps them understand that although there has been a separation, your love and attention for them remain the same.

Seek Mediation or Counseling: Mediation helps you and your ex-partner agree on how both of you will look after the children after the separation. The courts also encouraged mediation, as it is a faster way of resolving the problem without paying court fees. Separation can damage your self-confidence and disrupt your sense of identity. Counseling will help you cope with the situation by offering you different coping strategies and helping you get through difficult times and face those challenges head-on.

Staying Healthy: Looking after yourself and staying calm is the best way to ensure you can cope with the arduous task of getting your children back. It is a process that will require full concentration, motivation, and energy.

External Help: There are several resources you can leverage to get access to your children. Information is power, and getting this information will give you the confidence, courage, and strength you need throughout the process.

Coping Strategies: It is important to recognize that it is okay for you to have different feelings after a separation or divorce. During this time, you need to think positively, give yourself time to explore the things you have or want to do, give yourself a reasonable break, seek support, do the things that will help you emotionally and physically, and try to avoid getting into arguments with your ex-spouse. Thinking about the positive future of your children will give you the strength you need to overcome this.

What to Take Home from This Book

After a separation or divorce, children will ultimately become sad, angry, and frustrated and may feel uncertain about their future. Therefore, both parents must come to a compromise and facilitate contact to give the children the opportunity to get the required support for their development. Also, both parents must ensure that the interests of the children stay at the center of any decision they take to protect their future.

This book is designed to help parents who have been refused access to their children; it is designed to help them build resilience and fight back even when it seems like all hope is lost. The best way to raise a child is by giving them balanced support from both parents. Only then will they grow up to give their parents satisfaction and pride, and separation should not take that away from you.

It is important to understand that not every primary parent will prevent the alienating parent from having access to their children after a separation. Some primary parents are very understanding, and for the sake of the welfare of their children, they create a healthy space that enables the children to have access to the alienating parent regardless of what happened prior to the separation. It is important to maintain a peaceful environment after a separation, as this provides the opportunity for both parents to be involved in their children's upbringing. It is worth noting that a child is the main victim after a separation or divorce. As parents, it is important for us to consider the aftereffects of our decisions on the lives of our children.

Parental alienation is harmful to children and targeted parents. The problem is systemic in nature. Recognizing the warning signs and taking steps to prevent or mitigate its harmful effects is crucial for professionals and family members to support children and targeted parents and work toward combating parental alienation, building healthier and more stable family dynamics, and reuniting children with their parents.

Breaking the cycle of fatherless/motherless homes.

This book has set out to break the cycle of fatherless and motherless homes. It is to encourage both parent's involvement through early intervention after family separation. Reading his book will help parents suffering from long-term separation to find effective ways to reconnect with their children.

The author does not discriminate. He has written this book to support both fathers and mothers who have been affected by this problem.

Aims and Objectives:

- To promote equality for both parents, regardless of gender.
- To raise awareness of the effects of family separation.
- To lower the conflict between parents after separation through early intervention.

- To support families to avoid children being separated from their parents for prolonged periods.
- To encourage alienating parents' involvement by supporting them in reconnecting with their children.
- To support families struggling with co-parenting problems.
- To raise awareness of the need for children to have a loving relationship with both parents.
- Understanding parental alienation and its devastating effects on children and parents.
- Understanding that parental alienation is a silent epidemic that must be acknowledged and how appropriate support is provided to targeted parents and children.

I hope this book is beneficial to you. Should you need any further support or information, please do not hesitate to contact me through my email below.

Contact: nkomic@yahoo.com

Bisong Foundation: www.bisongfoundation.org.uk

YouTube: Bisong Foundation.

Sponsors Of This Book

My earnest thanks and gratitude go to the sponsors of this book.

Mrs Ann Holland & Sesekou Ayuk Manga:

Mrs Ann Holland is the CEO of Maofu Home and Community-based Services. This agency is renounced in its efforts of making a difference in the lives of individuals with developmental disabilities, mental health problems and mental retardation / Intellectual disability across the cities of Texas. The agency also has a reputation of providing great possibilities for individuals to engage in paid work or occupation that provides them with regular income. Mrs Holland has a robust and vibrant set of principles and associated talent practices that prioritize equality, inclusion, skills training, and opportunity for career advancement, within her agency while generating business value. Her 24-hour care is cost-friendly, efficient and reliable healthcare, which is serving the cities of Texas.

Mrs Ann Holland and her husband Sesekou Ayuk Manga have been integral in promoting the African culture, tradition and heritage in the US. They have practically taken part in the community events and offered both financial and moral support to several community groups. Their involvement to the groups has shaped a collective sense of peace and solidarity that is needed to stop conflict and build a peaceful community at large. Mrs Holland and her husband Sesekou Manga have been instrumental in the fight to alleviate poverty in Cameroon by marshalling resources in a bid to support vulnerable children and their families by providing them with living essentials they need to thrive, such as food, education and medical care.

Mrs Ann Holland can be contacted on +1 (210)-248-9336 / maofuhealth@gmail.com.

Mr Valentine Fominyam & Mrs Ashu Orock Fominyam:

Mrs Ashu Orock Fominyam and husband Mr Valentine Fominyam are both in the healthcare field. They owned and operates the Facility Destined Assisted Living located in Houston Texas where they are touching the lives of many residents.

They are also philanthropists and board members of Hadassah Foundation found in Buea, the Southwest Region of Cameroon. Hadassah Foundation is a charity organization that works to enhance the wellbeing of vulnerable groups (IDPs, orphans, street children, teenage girls, survivors of gender-based violence).

Mr and Mrs Fominyam with a heart for people, reach out to these groups in different ways ensuring that their basic needs are met. They are making a difference in the lives of Internally Displaced Persons (IDPs) in the Southwest region of Cameroon following the crisis. With their heart for children, Mr and Mrs Fominyam have opened their home as foster parents giving hope and love to different children in Houston Texas. They are also adoptive parents and are proud to have three lovely children a set of twin girls and a boy.

MANYU SISTERS ASSOCIATION HOUSTON - TEXAS:

Mrs Ashu Orock Fominyam is also the president of the Manyu Sisters Association Houston Texas USA.

This Association is made up of vibrant women of the Manyu Division of Cameroon by birth or Marriage and has as objective to:

I. Promote unity and respect amongst Manyu women.
II. II. Support each other socially and emotionally.
III. III. Share ideas that will benefit members and help us grow in every aspect of life.
IV. IV. To promote Manyu Culture.
V. V. To do profitable projects that will assist in the development of Manyu Division.

Mrs Jane Nyenty Senju & Mr Leke Senju:

Mrs Senju hails from Ntenako village in the Manyu Division of Cameroon. She is the viable president of Okoyong Past Student Association (UOPSA) and MOHWA HOUSTON. Her actions as well as her words, have resonated well within the souls of her kinswoman, making her a great leader. Mrs Senju is specialized in the health profession. Her career reflects her dedication to improving the health and wellbeing of individuals in the community of Houston and its surroundings, a trait which resonates well with her role as a community leader. The benefit of her career is the rewarding feeing of making a positive impact on people's lives which can be truly life changing.

Mrs Senju and her husband Mr Leke Senju are providing on-going financial and material support to many vulnerable and underprivileged people in and around their village in Cameroon, to make their lives better. They are providing this support in the form of philanthropy.

Mrs Glory Ako Tambe

Mrs Tambe is a philanthropist. She donates her time, experience, funds and skills to make life better for other people. She is driven by a deep desire to solve the problems of the people in her community, home and abroad. Her focus is on making the strongest impact that benefit as many people as possible through strategic philanthropic actions which involves supporting the cause that maters the most to the underprivileged and the best way of helping them. She has over the years funded educational programs, supported health initiative, including community improvement projects.

Mrs Tambe has continued to demonstrate several practical skills such as effective communication, problem-solving, empathy, and dedication in her profession. These skills have greatly contributed to the holistic care of individuals and communities. Her career reflects her dedication to the health and well-being of both children and vulnerable adults.

Okoyong Past Student Association (UOPSA) Houston, Texas - USA:

Mrs Jane Senju is the viable President of UOPSA Houston USA, a community group made up of vibrant women with valor, bonded with their infectious enthusiasm of love for one another. These women are quite exited, unique and optimistic about their future and that of a girl child. UOPSA strives to nurture a sense of belonging, empowerment and unity to their group and the community at large. The group enhances the personal and professional growth of its members, thus enabling them to succeed in their chosen domains. They are also strongly involved in community outreach programs. By collaborating with local organizations, the group participates efficiently and effectively in community services like; food - drive to the poor and needy, back to school projects for kids, and visiting battered women's shelter. Currently, the first back-home (Okoyong - Cameroon) projects are still in the pipeline. These projects will be executed by the end of this year 2024. The group ensures they give something back to their community and to Alma Mater. Thereby, fulfilling their ultimate Goal and practical commitment to Alma Mater.

UOPSA Motto "One love, One Heart".

Mme Vera Eben:

Mme Vera Eben is a philanthropist. She is responding to the immense needs of vulnerable children and families in Cameroon by providing social support which include food packages, finance, clothes and medication. This charitable action provides critical resources to the families as they break the circle of poverty and ensure a better future for their children. Be it in Cameroon or in the USA, her house has always been full because it is opened to everyone.

HRH Nfor Williams Bisong & Queen Regina Bisong-Esim:

HRH Nfor Williams Bisong of Manyemen and his wife have addressed the needs of the Manyemen people where we hail from. They have provided ongoing humanitarian support, love, hope, peace, and a sense of purpose of real lasting change to the people. They have ended the darkness and brought light to the people. They have done so by installing solar lights thereby providing access to electricity to the village. The most positive impact of access to solar lights which everyone has benefitted from in Manyemen, has been the increased sense of safety and security. They have organized community activities to bring the diverse community together to facilitate peace and unity and have created healthy social connections. HRH and wife have also been committed to end the water crisis and focus on reaching the entire Manyemen community, with access to clean pipe borne water.

Made in the USA
Columbia, SC
12 July 2025

f2247833-2bc0-4db7-bb43-c9a0ed0a079eR01